UNDER OUR ROOF

WRITTEN BY:
REBECCA STANTON

ILLUSTRATED BY:
KRISTY GAUNT

Under Our Roof / by Rebecca Stanton ; Illustrated by Kristy Gaunt

pages cm

ISBN 9781099023088 (US edition, paperback)
Imprint: Independently Published

Dedicated to my three children, who
inspire me and make me so proud.
Always be the best you can be.

- Mommy

UNDER OUR ROOF,

Love lives here everyday.

Love **LAUGHS** hard,
and Love likes to **PLAY**.

UNDER OUR ROOF,

Love is present on
sunny and cold days.

Love is what you **DO**,
and not what you **SAY**.

Love is shown
in different ways.

UNDER OUR ROOF,

Love is quality time,

movie nights, and big hugs.

UNDER OUR ROOF,

LOVE IS LO

UNDER OUR ROOF,

Love is saying
THANK YOU,

and **APOLOGIZING**
when you're mad.

UNDER OUR ROOF,

Love is **FORGIVING**.
It doesn't choose sides.

Love is all around us.
Love never hides.

UNDER OUR ROOF,

Love is armpit tickles,
and butterfly kisses.

Love is catching
fireflies in June,
and making
dandelion wishes.

UNDER OUR ROOF,

we love just like you.

Love knows no limit,
it reaches up to the sky.

UNDER OUR ROOF,

there's no end to its limit.

Love **ALWAYS** tries.

UNDER OUR ROOF,

Love is **UNLIMITED** and does not run out.

Love is
FAMILY.

Love is
FRIENDS.

It does
not judge.

UNDER OUR ROOF,

LOVE IS LO

UNDER OUR ROOF,

Love is yours,
and love is mine.

Love is **SILLY,**
and love is **KIND.**

UNDER OUR ROOF,

Love is having **TRADITIONS** and making **MEMORIES**.

It knows no boundaries.

UNDER OUR ROOF,

Love is having **TWO** mommies.

Made in the USA
Coppell, TX
29 May 2021

56537233R00019